YOUR LAND
AND
MY LAND
AFRICA

We Visit
RWANDA

John

Bankston

Mitchell Lane
PUBLISHERS

P.O. Box 196
Hockessin, Delaware 19707

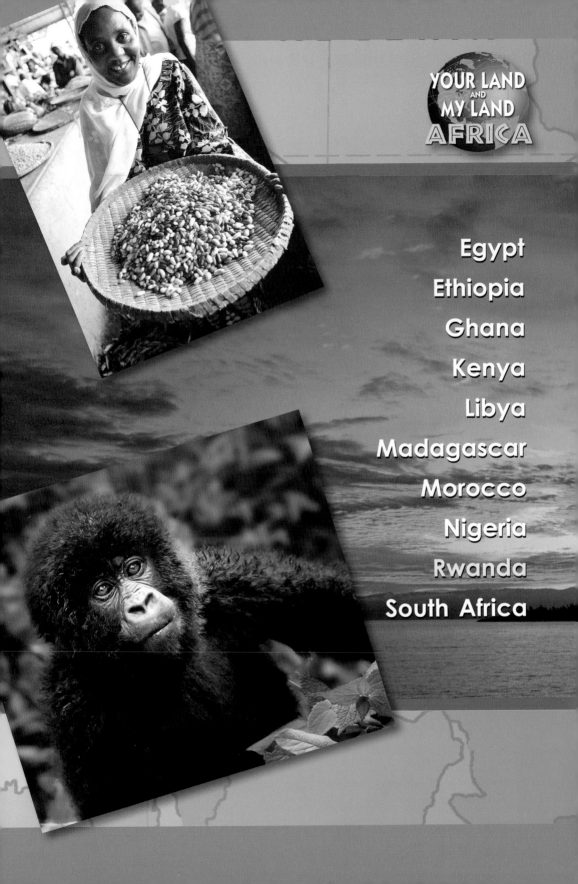

YOUR LAND
AND
MY LAND
AFRICA

Egypt

Ethiopia

Ghana

Kenya

Libya

Madagascar

Morocco

Nigeria

Rwanda

South Africa

LIBYA

EGYPT

Aswān.

YOUR LAND
AND
MY LAND
AFRICA

We Visit

RWANDA

SUDAN

Addis
Ababa
★

Mitchell Lane

PUBLISHERS

Printing   1   2   3   4   5   6   7   8   9

Library of Congress Cataloging-in-Publication to come
Bankston, John, 1974-
  We visit Rwanda / by John Bankston.
      p. cm. — (Your land and my land. Africa)
  Includes bibliographical references and index.
  ISBN 978-1-61228-307-4 (library bound)
  1. Rwanda—Juvenile literature. I. Title. II. Series: Your land and my land (Mitchell Lane Publishers). Africa.
  DT450.14.B36 2013
  967.571—dc23

                                                                    2012009881

eBook ISBN: 978161223814

PUBLISHER'S NOTE: This story is based on the author's extensive research, which he believes to be accurate. Documentation of this research is on page 61.

The internet sites referenced herein were active as of the publication date. Due to the fleeting nature of some websites, we cannot guarantee they will all be active when you are reading this book.

Contents

Introduction

The Great Lakes Region of Central Africa has been called paradise. Most of the region is over 3,200 feet (975 meters) above sea level. The mosquitoes and tsetse flies plaguing much of the continent rarely fly so high. Winds criss-crossing the region are damp, carrying moisture from low-lying clouds. This means rainfall is plentiful. It even rains during the "dry" seasons. Some African countries receive sufficient rain for growing crops, but their soil is not fertile enough to sustain them. Other places enjoy fertile soil, but not enough rainfall.

Located in the middle of the Great Lakes Region, Rwanda has both life-sustaining rain and fertile soil. The crops it grows, like coffee and bananas, are enjoyed by people across the world. Yet this is not what comes to mind when most people think about Rwanda. Nor do they remember famous naturalist Dian Fossey's study of the country's gorillas, which taught so many about the animal's true nature. Instead, when people think about Rwanda, they usually recall the horrific bloodshed endured by the country's people during a few months in the late spring and early summer of 1994.

Perhaps more than any other place on earth, Africa faces enormous challenges. North of Rwanda, political upheavals have toppled rulers like Muammar Gaddafi and Hosni Mubarak. Although millions in

Clouds mask a volcano in Rwanda

RWANDA

AFRICA

Libya and Egypt may enjoy new freedoms, they arrived at a cost of thousands of lives. In South Africa, a powerful minority once received the best schooling and jobs—until the majority overthrew them. This change in leadership was celebrated, but twenty years later, the nation's leaders still battle poverty and crime. And today along the Horn of Africa, millions face starvation in countries like Djibouti, South Sudan, Kenya, Ethiopia, and Uganda.

Rwanda faces similar challenges. Beginning in the early 1960s, the country's people overthrew its rulers. Afterward, the nation's majority —a group called the Hutu—battled against the minority Tutsi who enjoyed the best education and highest-paying careers. And today, decades of conflict have left many of Rwanda's poorest facing starvation.

Yet like the continent it calls home, Rwanda has advantages that may provide a path toward solutions. Like most other African nations, it was once ruled by a European country thousands of miles away. Today it is independent, just like fifty-six other countries in Africa. Having survived occupation by European colonizers, wars, and political upheavals, many believe the future for both the country and the continent is filled with promise.

Many residential districts in Rwanda's capital of Kigali were built alongside its famous hills. Its downtown area resembles many Western cities, filled with hotels, museums, and government buildings.

Land and Lakes

Welcome to Rwanda. You might be surprised to know that much of Rwanda's land is used for farming or raising cattle. Some 75 percent of the country's land is devoted to crops or pasture.

Rwanda is part of the Great Lakes Region of Central Africa, which includes the highlands of Burundi and the grasslands of western Tanzania and Uganda, stretching to the shores of Lake Victoria. It is also one of the most densely populated places on the continent. Over eleven million people are crammed into a country the size of Maryland —a state boasting fewer than six million residents.

Although most of the country is rural, it boasts one large city. The country's capital, Kigali, is also its most-populated city, with over one million people living there. Many of Rwanda's poor have moved there in search of jobs; government and embassy buildings crowd the down-town area alongside hotels for international travelers. Originally a military camp set up by the Germans in the early 20th century, Kigali rests on hills and valleys, which average about 5,000 feet (1,500 meters) above sea level. It still offers numerous markets that attract buyers and sellers from across the region.

The Virunga Mountains form a continental divide between the Nile and Congo River basins. The range features numerous volcanoes. While active volcanoes like Nyiragongo and Nyamuragira are located in the neighboring Democratic Republic of the Congo, they are sometimes heard and felt in Rwanda. The volcanoes in Rwanda have long been dormant, but once they spewed so much smoke and ash that they could alter the weather.

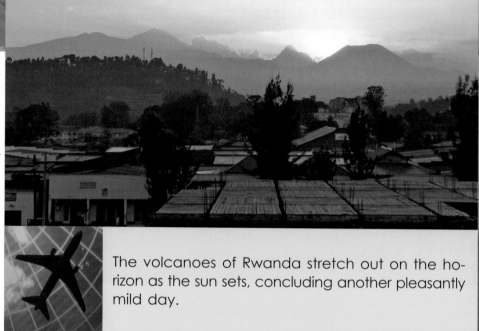

The volcanoes of Rwanda stretch out on the horizon as the sun sets, concluding another pleasantly mild day.

Along the equator, the tropics of South America and the dry savanna of Africa can get extremely hot. Sunrise and sunset occur quickly. There are about twelve hours of sunlight almost every day. It doesn't matter what the calendar says—it feels like summer.

The equator also cuts across the Great Lakes Region, but because of its elevation, it doesn't get hot like other equatorial regions. Just south of the equator, Rwanda's elevation ranges from 3,117 feet (950 meters) all the way up to 14,826 feet (4,519 meters) atop Mount Karisimbi. Air pressure is lower at higher altitudes, which results in air temperatures being cooler than they are at lower-lying land near the equator.

To the west of Rwanda is the Democratic Republic of the Congo (formerly Zaire). The boundary between the two countries is marked

FYI FACT:

There are four seasons in Rwanda. *Urugaryi* is a short, dry season in January and February, followed by *itumba*, the heavy rainy season beginning in March and ending in May. *Ikyi* is the long, dry season running from June to September, and *umuhindo* is the short rainy season that lasts from October to December.

WHERE IN THE WORLD IS RWANDA?

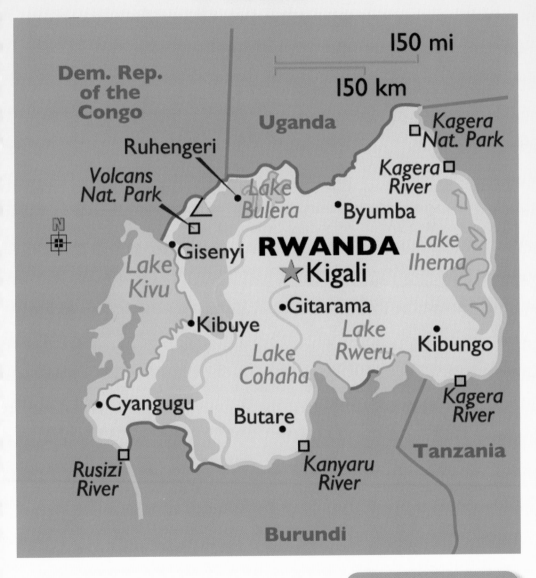

150 mi

150 km

Dem. Rep. of the Congo

Uganda

Kagera Nat. Park

Ruhengeri

Kagera River

Volcans Nat. Park

Lake Bulera

•Byumba

N

•Gisenyi **RWANDA**

Lake Ihema

Lake Kivu

★Kigali

•Gitarama

•Kibuye

Lake Rweru

Kibungo

Lake Cohaha

•Cyangugu

Butare

Kagera River

Rusizi River

Kanyaru River

Tanzania

Burundi

Where in the World

11

Lake Kivu

in part by Lake Kivu. Stretching some 60 miles (97 kilometers) between Congo and Rwanda, it is a popular destination for vacationers. The lake is also safer to swim and boat in than many other African lakes, because there are no crocodiles or hippos here.

Forests and lakes lie along Rwanda's southern border with Burundi, while its eastern border contains savannas that are common to its eastern neighbor, Tanzania. Uganda borders Rwanda to the north; the northern part of Rwanda includes the Virunga volcanoes. Their ancient eruptions helped produce some of the richest soil on earth.

It is a soil ideal for pyrethrum, a flower used as an insecticide for growing foods like coffee and bananas. Bananas are one of the country's most fruitful crops—few places on the continent are so ideal as Rwanda. They grow best where the temperature is warm, but rainfall is consistent. Unlike many other African countries, Rwanda doesn't endure long dry spells.

Bananas are easier to grow than other native African crops like yams and sorghum. Even better, while many crops might barely feed the farmer and his family, most banana farmers enjoy surpluses—there is enough to eat and sell. The average person in the United States eats 25 pounds (11 kilograms) of bananas a year—that's about a banana a week. In Rwanda, people eat as much as 500 pounds (225 kilograms) a year!

There's more than bananas in Rwanda. The country is also home to a variety of animals that benefit from its temperate climate and stable food supply.

RWANDA FACTS AT A GLANCE

Rwandan flag

Full name: Republic of Rwanda

Official languages: Kinyarwanda, French, English

Population: 11,689,696 (July 2012 est.)

Land area: 9,524 square miles (24,668 square kilometers); slightly smaller than Maryland

Capital: Kigali

Government: republic; presidential, multiparty system

Ethnic makeup: Hutu 84%, Tutsi 15%, Twa 1%

Religions: Roman Catholic 56.5%, Protestant 26%, Adventist 11.1%, Muslim 4.6%, indigenous beliefs 0.1%, none 1.7%

Exports: coffee, tea, hides, tin ore

Imports: foodstuffs, machinery and equipment, steel, petroleum products, cement and construction material

Crops: coffee, tea, pyrethrum, bananas, beans, sorghum, potatoes

Average high temperatures: Kigali: April 75°F (24°C); September 81°F (27°C)

Average annual rainfall: Kigali: 39.6 inches (100.7 centimeters)

Highest point: Mount Karisimbi—14,826 feet (4,519 meters)

Lowest point: Rusizi River—3,117 feet (950 meters)

Longest river: Kagera River—430 miles (692 kilometers)

Description of flag: Three horizontal bands of sky blue (top, double width), yellow, and green, with a golden sun with twenty-four rays near the fly end of the blue band; blue represents happiness and peace, yellow economic development and mineral wealth, green hope of prosperity and natural resources; the sun symbolizes unity, as well as enlightenment and transparency from ignorance.

National sport: There is no official national sport, although football (soccer) is popular.

National anthem: "Rwanda Nziza" (Rwanda, Our Beautiful Country)

Sources:

CIA World Factbook: Rwanda

Republic of Rwanda: "National Symbols," http://www.gov.rw/National-Symbols

Although the mountain gorillas of Rwanda are humans' distant relatives, they were once hunted to near-extinction by poachers. Today, they are a source of national pride and profit as tourists travel from across the globe to see them.

Native Animals

Ten thousand feet (3,000 meters) above sea level, thick mist cloaks the ground along the Virunga Mountain Range. In the Democratic Republic of the Congo, volcanoes belch smoke and ash, their deep rumblings warning of possible eruptions. Just across the border in Rwanda, the volcanoes are dormant, the food supply abundant. Yet despite this, some of the country's best-known residents struggle for survival.

Few people from Rwanda are as famous as the mountain gorillas there. They adorn postcards and book covers, they star in documentaries and television commercials. Going to see them requires a U.S. $750 permit.

Observing these animals, it is easy to notice how they resemble people. They spend less time in trees than chimpanzees, and more time walking. Their big hands and feet resemble our own. Baby gorillas behave like human infants—exploring, playing, and putting just about everything they find into their mouths. The dark eyes of mountain gorillas appear thoughtful and intelligent; even the youngest have faces which seem both ancient and wise.

In small groups, mountain gorillas are led by the silverback. This is the dominant male, who has lived long enough that the hairs along his back have turned gray. Gorillas can live to be fifty years old and female gorillas usually have between two to six offspring during their lifetime.

Once mountain gorillas were feared. Comics and movies featured gorillas attacking, even eating people. In fact, they are essentially vegetarians—the only meat they eat comes from small insects. Instead, they eat over one hundred different types of plants. Dining exclusively on vegetables doesn't keep them from getting big—some males grow to more than 6 feet (183 centimeters) tall and over 400 pounds (180 kilograms). They are also far stronger than humans of the same size.

Dian Fossey's first meeting with Louis Leakey did not go well. The world-famous paleontologist treated her like a tourist, charging her for visiting his excavation site. While she was there, Fossey broke both her ankle and a fossil he'd uncovered. It didn't matter. In a few years, Leakey would change Fossey's life.

Fossey loved animals. She dreamed of being a veterinarian until failing grades in several science courses altered that ambition. In 1963, she was in her early thirties when she traveled to Africa and met Leakey. After her money ran out, she returned home to the U.S.

Fossey was living in Kentucky when Leakey visited the state three years later. Following his lecture, she approached him. He didn't just remember her. He offered her a job.

Leakey wanted Fossey to return to Africa and observe mountain gorillas. She didn't believe she was the right person for the job: she didn't have any training, she was too old, she was a woman. But Leakey wasn't looking for an over-trained candidate. He believed she was the perfect age, and that women were more patient and quiet— ideal for spending long hours watching gorillas.

Returning to Africa, Fossey did not expect to change how people saw gorillas. But she did. She lived in Zaire (now the Democratic

Dian Fossey

On June 16, 2012, the eighth annual gorilla-naming ceremony took place. This popular festival attracts thousands of tourists, conservationists, and reporters to Volcanoes National Park. In 2012, the festival celebrated the births of nineteen gorillas and the naming of an adult female gorilla. The *Kwita Izina* ceremony is one of the ways Rwanda has worked to preserve this endangered species. Even people who are unable to travel to the country can see pictures of baby gorillas and vote for the cutest in the "Gorilla Idol Contest." The 2012 ceremony theme of "Sustainable Tourism For a Green Economy," reflects the Rwandan government's goal of preserving this endangered species and attracting tourists who spend money to see gorillas—unlike the visitors of the 1900s who wanted to hunt them.

Republic of the Congo) for several years before a revolution drove her to Rwanda. There she built a campsite in Volcanoes National Park.

Focusing on fifty-one gorillas in four groups, Fossey did not just observe them. She imitated their behavior and learned to speak their "language"—mimicking grunts which they used to communicate. Several of them became comfortable enough with her to sit beside her —one even held her hands. When they became threatened by poachers, she fought back. When one of her favorite gorillas was killed, she became more aggressive. She destroyed traps, and frightened and arrested poachers.

Fossey's films, writings, and lectures changed people's perceptions. Because of her work, people realized gorillas weren't dangerous beasts, but were instead shy and nearly human in their behavior. The Rwandan government once seemed indifferent to their survival. Local hunters killed mountain gorillas without fear of arrest.

Today tourists from all over the world visit Rwanda and spend millions of dollars just for a chance to catch a glimpse of a mountain gorilla. Instead of ignoring poaching, today the government doesn't even allow tourists with colds in the park because the primates can catch human diseases. Dian Fossey never witnessed these changes. Sometime around Christmas in 1985, she was murdered. Her killer may have been a poacher—no one was ever charged with the crime. She was fifty-three.

Mountain gorillas are perfectly suited to their environment. Their home is cold and damp, but their fur is thick. They don't even need to drink water—they get enough from plants. Despite this, mountain gorillas are almost extinct. This means in a few years there might not be any mountain gorillas left.

Today only a few hundred remain. Poachers have killed them for their body parts, and baby gorillas have been taken alive—but for each young gorilla taken, half-a-dozen or more protective gorillas may be killed in the process.

Mountain gorillas survive in protected places like Volcanoes National Park, which is run by the government. Because mountain gorillas do not survive long in captivity, the park offers visitors their best chance to see them.

Visitors usually come to Volcanoes National Park for the gorillas, but the park offers a chance to see other animals as well. Primates are an order of mammals which includes gorillas and people. While the gorilla is a large primate, visitors watching the golden monkey push through dense strands of bamboo will see a primate that weighs about as much as a house cat (between 10 and 25 pounds or 4 and 11 kilograms). Golden fur decorates its body, cheeks, and tail. Comfortable being watched by tourists, they are often seen playing in the open glades.

Volcanoes National Park traces its history to 1925. A far newer park, the Nyungwe Forest National Park near Lake Kivu, was established in 2004. Within the park's bamboo, rainforest, grassland, and swamps are an extraordinary array of plants, animals, and birds. There are thirteen different primate species, including chimpanzees. Great blue turacos, birds that are roughly the size of chickens, flit about on bright blue, green, and yellow feathers.

The animals of the savanna are regularly featured in nature films. Although this dry, grassy landscape is more common in Tanzania and Kenya, Rwanda has its own area of savanna. Akagera National Park, named after the river running along its eastern boundary, is lower and

A hippo in Akagera
National Park

hotter than most of the country. Buffaloes, elephants, zebras, and antelopes are often seen by park visitors. Some camp beside the park's lakes, even though the waters are teeming with crocodiles and hippos.

Today, fewer wild animals survive outside of protected parks. Even within the shelter of the parks, poaching kills numerous elephants, gorillas, and other animals every year. The story of why they disappeared is the story of Rwanda. Like its people, animals face both death and the destruction of their homes. Clearing the land for farms and pastures, or cutting down trees for fuel in the short term may help a few Rwandans. Yet this destruction ultimately harms both animals and people.

"The natural forest cover of Rwanda has been almost completely stripped by decades of subsistence agriculture and fuel wood cutting," explains scientist Kenneth LaPensee. "The depletion of the environment damaged the land to the point where scarcity precipitated one of the most widespread and brutal genocides in human history."[1]

Mountain gorillas were once feared, but people have less to fear from them than they do from us. Gorillas thrived millions of years before human beings walked the earth. Today, many scientists believe these powerful primates are our distant relatives. Their extinction would be a death in the family.

Today, Mount Sabyinyo is an extinct volcano located at the intersection of the borders of Uganda, Rwanda, and the Congo. But over twenty million years ago, like many other volcanoes in the Virunga Range, it was active, with eruptions contributing to the development of lakes, increased elevation, and fertile soil in the region.

Beginnings

Our world was a vastly different place hundreds of millions of years ago. But ninety-seven percent of Africa hasn't moved in over 300 million years. Since then, its shape has scarcely changed.

Every continent on Earth was once connected. In a place called Pangaea, Africa was the anchor. Then, about 175 million years ago, the North and South American, Eurasian, Antarctic, and Australian continental plates began to drift apart. They formed the major continents of planet Earth. Today, their coasts resemble enormous puzzle pieces. Millions of years after their separation from Africa, it is still possible to see where they once fit together.

Forces below the surface pushed together other continental plates. Africa was pulled. The continent was stretched, creating one of its most distinctive features. The 3,700-mile (6,000-kilometer) long Great Rift Valley is a deep trench. Millions of years from now, it will split the entire continent in two.

Beneath the surface of the Great Rift Valley, rocks are molten— liquid and flowing from the extreme heat. The Virunga Range illustrates what happens when molten rock explodes through the surface: volcanoes. Twenty to thirty million years ago, earthquakes and volcanoes began to produce Rwanda's lakes and fertile soils.

East of the valley, much of the landscape is dry—either semi-arid desert or grassy savanna. To the west of the valley, including Rwanda, are mountains and forests: areas where the land's height is an advantage and rain is plentiful.

Anthropologists study human beings going back to our oldest ancestors. Most of them believe that modern humans are close cousins to gorillas and chimpanzees. "Humans are so closely related to the apes that more than 99 percent of our DNA is identical to that of the chimpanzee," explains John Reader in his book *Africa.* "This means that chimpanzees and humans diverged from their common ancestor only in the recent past. The common ancestor lived between seven and five million years ago in the luxuriant forests to the west of the Rift Valley."[1]

This area probably included Rwanda. The common ancestor—the so-called missing link—has never been found. Scientists are not certain why some of its offspring slowly evolved or changed over time. Some became the gorillas which now live in the country's densely wooded mountains. Others evolved into human beings.

To find evidence of this, we must leave Rwanda and head east across the Great Rift Valley to where Tanzania and Kenya are today. The hot and grassy savanna is where early man evolved.

The savannas of eastern Rwanda seem out of place in the country, more closely resembling the landscapes of Tanzania and Kenya that receive little rain.

Hominid fossils

Homo neanderthalensis

Homo neanderthalensis

Human Evolution

With thick brow ridges over their eyes and hairy, stumpy bodies, they resembled short gorillas more than modern people. They weren't as fast or as strong as the dangerous animals stalking the countryside. But they were smarter.

From humble beginnings, these early people—called hominids— began changing. Body hair diminished. More often, they stood upright and walked on two legs. Their arms became shorter, even as their brains grew larger.

This process of slow change is called evolution. Anthropologists believe it took millions of years for early people called *Australopithecus* to become *Homo erectus* ("upright man"), *Homo habilis* ("handy man"), and eventually today's modern man, *Homo sapiens* ("wise man").

Homo erectus were the first to range far from their home, using a land bridge to cross from Africa into Asia. *Homo habilis* was the first to use tools, while *Homo erectus* conquered fire. More important than providing heat for cooking and warmth, fire kept dangerous animals away.

Homo sapiens lived in eastern Africa over 100,000 years ago. Fossils —bones and other material which were preserved over time—suggest that humans did not reach the Great Lakes Region of Africa until thousands of years later.

 Descending from early quadrupedal primates, *Homo sapiens* first appeared in eastern Africa over 100,000 years ago.

One theory explains this. Even as early humans were changing, so too was the environment which supported them. The world grew colder. Ice expanded from beyond the north and south poles around 100,000 years ago until it covered the land of present-day countries like Canada and Great Britain. Most of Africa was spared. Still, the weather was altered for thousands of years.

The upper elevations of Rwanda were probably icy; it was certainly colder. Worse than the temperature was the lack of rain. It has never been as dry in Africa as it was during the last major ice age. At its peak some 20,000 years ago, the earth was further from the sun year round. Because of this, one-third of the land on the planet became covered in ice. Much of the rest turned to desert. The oceans and seas around Africa became frigid.

When the ice finally receded and the oceans warmed, rainfall increased. Lakes and rivers returned. Forests grew, spreading across the Virunga Mountains. The region became the place familiar to travelers today, described by one writer who says, "If the Garden of Eden ever existed on Earth, it should have been in the Great Lakes region of Central Africa."[2]

FYI FACT:

Rwanda's first archaeological exhibits were displayed following a visit from the King of Belgium in 1955; over thirty years later, the National Museum of Rwanda was created. Eighty miles (130 kilometers) from Rwanda's capital, the museum in Butare is located on 50 acres (20 hectares) of land. Inside, a visitor can find everything from maps and photos to historic farming tools and traditional clothing. One room is devoted to prehistoric Rwanda, based on both the stories handed down from generation to generation and written documents. Exploring the displays, visitors can experience what life was like in Rwanda hundreds, or even thousands of years ago.

When the first hunter-gatherers made their homes alongside the dense rainforests of the Congo, they relied on the plants and animals provided by the land to survive.

Chapter 4

The People of Rwanda

Sometime between 20,000 and 50,000 years ago, the first hunter-gatherers settled beside the dense rainforests of the Congo Basin. They lived on the plants they could find and the animals they could kill. Even today, it is not easy to survive there. The Congo Basin includes portions of Rwanda. Located between the Gulf of Guinea and the African Great Lakes, it contains some of the largest rainforests in Africa. The land of India, a country of over one billion people, could fit within its borders. Only about 80 million people live in the Congo Basin, although that number is quickly growing.

Historically, the people who lived in the forests of the Congo Basin were quite short—the men rarely taller than five feet (152 centimeters), the women a few inches shorter. This was an advantage. Smaller people need less food. In the heat and humidity, they cooled faster. In the rainforest, the trees grew so close together that their leaves nearly blocked out the sun. The people's size enabled them to move through the forest more easily.

These early arrivals were ancestors of a group once called Pygmies. Today, these people are more accurately classified by their tribe or ethnic group. One of these groups is the Twa. Their earliest descriptions came from an expedition organized by Egypt's King Neferkare over 4,000 years ago. Writing from central Africa, an explorer described

Once called Pygmies, the Twa of Rwanda are known for their short stature and talents for living in areas where most people cannot.

the Pygmies as "a dancing dwarf of the god from the land of the spirits." In the 1800s, one German said they were "remnants of a declining race." Today only one out of every one hundred Rwandans is Twa.[1]

The history of the country's three main groups is both confusing and complex. For some time, many believed the hunter-gatherer Twa were displaced by Hutu farmers. The Twa were forced to move deep into the forests. Later, the Tutsi—cattle herders—conquered the Hutu.

This theory implies that Hutu ancestors entered the country all at once. Instead, recent evidence suggests the arrivals came steadily over time.

Modern Hutu are related to the Bantu farmers who began migrating across sub-Saharan Africa about 3,000 years ago. Their arrival in the Great Lakes Region and elsewhere transformed societies of hunter-gatherers into agricultural communities. This was a more settled life that allowed populations to grow and cities to develop.

The Bantu who settled in the Great Lakes Region most likely came from the west, probably the area that is the modern-day country of Cameroon. They developed a talent for iron smelting—where iron ore was heated and crafted into tools and weapons. This craft required charcoal produced from trees—a lot of trees. After clearing the trees for charcoal, they planted on the denuded forest.

The Hutu began to arrive in Rwanda around the 5th century C.E., altering the lives of the Twa. Initially, the Twa helped the Hutu clear the forest. As the Hutu became established, the Twa provided them with meat and honey in exchange for crops like corn and bananas. The Hutu were generally peaceful. Mountains and thick forest kept most outsiders away, but the Hutu and Twa were unprepared for the Tutsi.

Migrating from a region near the Nile River, perhaps Egypt or Ethiopia, the Tutsi spoke a Nilotic language. Like the rulers of the Nile regions, the Tutsi king was mummified after death. Tutsis began arriving after 1300 C.E.; by then the Hutu and Twa spoke a common language. The Tutsi were generally taller than the Hutu, often over six feet (183 centimeters) tall, and very lean. Pastoralists, they raised livestock like cattle, and considered farmers lower class. The Tutsi culture was based on conquest. Led by a warrior king, Tutsi lives were punctuated with battles and the beats of drums adorned with the skins of slaughtered rivals.

A popular theory about the Tutsi proposes that they overpowered the Hutu and seized their farms because they needed land for their cattle. But evidence suggests that the Twa, Hutu, and Tutsi worked together for hundreds of years.

The clan system protected clan members—in exchange, they were expected to pay the clan's leader by either giving them a share of the crops raised or cattle. There were a few major clans and numerous

Tutsi and Hutu children play
together in the village of Kibago.

minor ones. They included not just Tutsis, but Hutu and Twa members as well.

In the 15th and 16th centuries, the major clans evolved into kingdoms headed by a Tutsi *Mwami* or king. Sometime in the 1600s, Mwami Ruganzu Ndori founded the Nyiginya Kingdom when he conquered central Rwanda, including areas ruled by the Hutu. Although Tutsi nobles advised the king, there were also Hutu advisors. In other parts of Rwanda, Hutus and Tutsis oversaw their areas under the control of the Tutsi king.

Still, most important jobs were held by the Tutsi. The king oversaw local Tutsi chiefs who ruled smaller territories within the kingdom. The Twa were used as jesters—forced into playing the fool for the royal court's entertainment.

Centuries later, European colonizers would see the Tutsi as the superior group in Rwanda. They placed them in charge and gave them the best jobs and education. This slight would feed the anger of the Hutu majority population.

The story of the Tutsi invasion and their domination over the Hutu has recently been questioned by anthropologists. For one thing, the supposedly obvious differences between them don't exist. The Tutsi are generally tall and lean, while Hutus are short and stocky, but intermarriage between them was common. Over time, this diminished their physical differences. Class differences were not clearly fixed either. Sometimes a Tutsi would lose his cattle and turn to farming to survive. When this happened he was no longer considered Tutsi, but Hutu. Hutu could also advance by increasing the number of cattle they owned. In many places, Tutsis had few advantages over the Hutu.

Despite their differences, the Hutu, Tutsi, and Twa have many things in common. They lived beside each other for centuries; their lives were interconnected. The Twa traded with the Hutu, while the Hutu raised cattle provided by the Tutsi. Over hundreds of years, their distinct languages evolved into a common tongue: Kinyarwanda. Their traditions also have much in common.

These young Intore—"the chosen"—are well-trained dancers who reenact Tutsi battles.

Culture Beats

On holidays and during ceremonies, the dance would begin. The dancers were young Tutsi men known as the *Intore*—"the chosen." Part celebration, part intimidation of rivals, the dance was fierce. Garbed in elaborate yellow grass headdresses swung loosely like long hair, the Intore reenacted battles, leaping and twisting, a short spear grasped in their hand.

They moved to the beat of the drummers who were as carefully selected and trained as the dancers. Village chiefs competed with their own drummers and dancers, while selected children were given a top education in warfare and became members of the king's celebrated dance troupe. Hundreds of years ago, they performed before royalty.

There was an expression in Rwanda: "He is king who has the drums." The *Kalinga* was the royal sacred drum, the king's drum. Beginning around 1600 C.E. when the Nyiginya Kingdom was founded, the Kalinga became a symbol of the king's power.

Traditionally, the Kalinga was placed in the center and it was encircled by two dozen lesser royal drums, the *ingabe*. Moving around the tall drums, drummers hit each in turn so that every drum was played including the Kalinga. The performances were reserved for special occasions like the beginning of planting season and only rarely seen by the average citizen.

Today the drums have changed—they are no longer made of zebra skin, but from cowhide instead. The drummers have changed as well —now women are allowed to play.

Although the Intore were Tutsi, Rwandans share many cultural traditions. Rosamond Halsey Carr was a young New Jersey bride when she moved to Africa in 1949. By 1956, she was divorced and managing a pyrethrum plantation, one of the first women to do so. Her observations on Rwandans came from living in the country for over forty years. "Despite the physical differences and social distinctions," she wrote in her memoir, *Land of a Thousand Hills,* the Tutsi, Hutu, and Twa "shared similar cultural customs with respect to courtship, marriage, family structure, and how they conducted their lives."[2] These customs affect almost every activity, from marriage and childbirth to death.

After getting married, a traditional Rwandan bride would only see her husband, her mother, and her bridesmaids for thirty days. After marriage, the couple usually lived close to the parents of the groom in a family compound. Simple homes once had thatched roofs and were made from the closest available materials. The homes were surrounded by hedges or fences beside a plot of land which was often a banana grove. A collection of family compounds located on a single hill formed "the hill," which was governed by a chief who answered to the king.

Until 1950 it was legal for a man to have several wives so long as he could afford them. Each wife lived in her own house. Although Rwanda is still mainly rural, today many Tutsi have moved to the cities. The traditional hill lifestyle is Hutu-dominated.

A modern bride and groom attend their dowry ceremony. At this ceremony, the groom's family pays a dowry to the bride's family, often in cattle.

Other traditions include the time when a woman rests in her home after giving birth—four days for a girl, five for a boy. One week after the child's birth is the naming ceremony. Friends and family gather to suggest names for the baby, and at the end of the ceremony, the parents announce their decision. Every child has three names—a family name, a Rwandan name, and a religious name.

Enjoying a meal in a traditional Rwandan home is filled with surprises. The first is the seating arrangements. Only adult men enjoy chairs, while women and children sit on the floor atop mats. Guests are always offered food; refusing to eat is a terrible insult. Guests also sit on chairs and eat with the men—first. Women and children wait until the men are finished. The Rwandan host helps his guest feel comfortable by tasting each dish first. This assures the guest that the meal has not been poisoned.

Most Hutus can't drink milk without getting sick, but it is an important part of many Tutsis' diets. Meat is a rare luxury reserved for special occasions in most Hutu homes. In the past, Rwandan women would not eat goat. Goats were considered stubborn animals with harsh "voices" and beards; Rwandans believed that if a woman ate a goat, she would behave like one. Many Rwandans still believe this today, and will not serve goat to a woman. Women are also not supposed to cut the grass, roof a hut, or walk under a spear.

In the United States, just before leaving a relative's home, one is usually offered something to take along—a pie perhaps, or a plate of ham. In Rwanda, they always make sure the guest leaves with something as well.

Until recently, large meals were always eaten at home. Tradition forbade eating at a restaurant. Even special occasions like weddings did not offer full meals. Instead, meat and a side dish like potatoes were offered. Drinks came from a large pot of sorghum beer placed in the center of the table. This beer, made from a type of grain, is usually served at room temperature. Instead of cups, guests drank from reed straws which were placed in the pot.

Today, many Rwandans enjoy the same activities they have enjoyed for centuries. A popular board game called mancala or igisoro has a long and not completely understood history. It is played with a wooden board with hollowed-out holes containing beans. These beans are then moved very quickly from hole to hole until one player's beans are eliminated. Boards can be very elaborate and are often hand-carved. Beads, buttons, and a variety of other objects are often used instead of beans. Many children use marbles.

As in many countries across the world, football (soccer) is the most popular team sport in Rwanda. But people enjoy many other activities, as well. In Kigali, the Cercle Sportif offers tennis and squash courts along with swimming pools and basketball facilities. There is also an eighteen-hole golf course nearby.

The traditions of the Hutu, the Tutsi, and the Twa have endured for centuries. Even after the arrival of Europeans in the 1800s, many aspects of their culture remained unchanged.

The popular board game igisoro has been played for centuries across Rwanda and in other African countries like Kenya, where another variation of the game is called bao.

The Belgian quest for a colony began as King Leopold I's search for a place to send his country's poor population. Later, his son realized that the Congo was filled with a valuable resource—rubber.

Arrival of
the Colonials

Belgium is a tiny country and half a world away from Rwanda. But despite its size and location, it was the leader in the "scramble for Africa," the contest among European nations to gain control of Africa's resources. The decisions made by Belgium had an enormous and tragic impact on Rwandans in the 20th century.

Belgium's King Leopold I had a problem. The collapse of the flax industry combined with a food shortage and an outbreak of disease had impoverished much of his country. The poor were turning to crime, preferring to be put in jail, where at least they received food and shelter. The king had an interesting solution. He planned to send them to another country. The only question was where.

The king hoped to purchase a colony, land he would control that would provide natural resources and a place for some of Belgium's poor to live. The government refused to fund King Leopold I's dreams. So with his own money he tried to buy Crete from Turkey, the Faeroe Islands from Denmark—he even tried to buy part of Texas! No one would sell to him; he made fifty-one unsuccessful attempts to buy a colony during his reign. In 1865, Leopold I died, passing on the throne to his son, Leopold II. The new king was just as eager to have a colony of his own.

By this time, a number of European countries had sent explorers into Africa. Along with missionaries, who converted natives to Christianity, the explorers wrote about their experiences.

In 1862, when John Hanning Speke encountered the Tutsi, he was the first European to do so. He'd traveled to the Great Lakes Region, one of the last areas of Africa explored by outsiders. His assumptions endured for a century. "In these countries," he wrote, "the government is in the hands of foreigners, who had invaded and taken possession of them, leaving the agricultural aborigines to till the ground, whilst the junior members of the usurping clans herded cattle."[1]

His belief that the Tutsi were not only superior but clearly from somewhere else was described in the chapter: "Theory of Conquest of Inferior by Superior Races." It was worse than just wrong. It would affect the lives of the Hutu and the Tutsi for over a century.

At the Brussels Geographic Conference in 1876, King Leopold II told attendees that Europeans needed to go to Africa "to open up to civilization the only part of our globe which it has not yet penetrated, to pierce the darkness in which entire populations are enveloped." He told them, "the tide is with us... in bringing you to Brussels I have not been influenced by selfish views."[2]

Afterward the twenty-four explorers, politicians, businessmen, and others from various European countries, along with thirteen Belgians, helped set up the International African Association (IAA) to bring "civilization" to Africa. King Leopold II was elected its president. In less than a decade, his true ambitions revealed themselves.

Reporter Henry Morton Stanley became famous for tracking down missing explorer David Livingstone. When he found him along the shores of Lake Tanganyika in East Africa, Stanley's greeting, "Doctor Livingstone, I presume," would become famous. By 1879, Stanley was overseeing the construction of roads and settlements in the Congo. The project was financed by King Leopold II and organized by the IAA.

By 1885, when the Berlin Conference offered sections of Africa to various European countries, Belgium set its sights on the Congo. Neighboring Rwanda was initially part of German East Africa. African natives were not consulted.

By the 1890s, solid rubber bicycle tires were being replaced by tires with a new inflatable design. The high wheel bicycle with its oversized

Not all native Rwandan culture revolves around music and dance. Prior to the arrival of Europeans, their religious beliefs were centered on the land. Special ceremonies paid respect to the most powerful of the *abazima*, or ancestors. Rwandans believed in a supreme god, *Imana*, who spoke through the abazima, lesser gods, and the king. The king's access to God made him responsible for the nation's fate. Neglecting deceased ancestors brought evil spirits upon the living. All bad luck was once believed to come from evil spirits.

front tire, considered the perfect transportation for a "gentleman," was out of style. Replacing it was a new "safety bicycle" that was appropriate for everyone. The demand for rubber was growing, and King Leopold's land in the Congo was filled with rubber trees. By this point, the king had found other places to ship his poorest citizens. He planned to use the resources of the Congo for profit.

In 1894, German Count Gustav Adolf van Goetzen traveled to what is now Rwanda. He led a wave of missionaries in the area.

Gustav Adolf van Goetzen

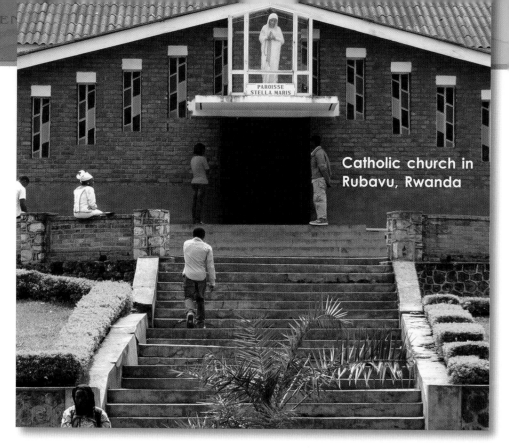

Catholic church in Rubavu, Rwanda

Their success is evidenced by the fact that the majority of Rwandans today are Catholic.

By the late 1890s, the Germans had begun indirect rule in Rwanda, using the social structure that appeared to be in place already. They were met with little resistance, and relied on the Tutsi to administer German East Africa. Their time in the country, however, was relatively brief. By 1916, Germany was fighting in World War I when the Belgian military drove the Germans out of Rwanda. After Germany's defeat, the League of Nations gave the region to Belgium, and it was renamed Ruanda-Urundi.

The League of Nations expected Belgium to only govern Rwanda until its own people could govern it. Belgian leaders believed the Tutsi were best suited for the task and began giving them incredible power. Tutsis were given the best jobs. Because they believed the Hutu weren't as smart as the Tutsi, only Tutsi children were allowed to attend school. Since it wasn't easy to tell who was Tutsi and who was Hutu, by the 1930s the Belgian Government required that every Rwandan have an identity card. The law mandated that anyone who owned ten or more cows was Tutsi, any less and he was Hutu.

In many other African countries, foreigners enjoyed the best farm land and owned the most successful plantations. Not in Rwanda. Under Belgian control, the amount of land which could be foreign-owned was limited. Still, a large foreign population settled in the area around Lake Kivu. Besides Belgians, there were people from France, Poland, Austria, Italy, and England.

In the 1600s, after Tutsi King Ruganzu Ndori established the Nyiginya Kingdom, a system developed. The elite, the *shebuja,* were the richest in the kingdom. Usually, but not always, they were Tutsi. They lent their cattle to herdsmen in exchange for their labor and political support. The shebuja also offered protection to the herdsmen in the case of a dispute. This system of *buhake* continued for several centuries. Under Belgian control, the system was given the power of law; even worse, many Tutsi used it to take cattle from rivals.

Despite its horrors, the conclusion of World War II in 1945 altered the lives of many Africans who had lived under colonial occupation. British forces had helped liberate countries whose leaders had killed millions of their own citizens. Many began to question how Britain could free so many people, but still keep far-away colonies under its control. France and Belgium had suffered under Nazi occupation, how could they so easily return to being occupiers?

Besides the question of right or wrong, there was also the cost. It was expensive to manage a colony thousands of miles away—something the British first learned by their ill-fated attempt to manage a colony which became the United States of America. For the natives of African countries, the outcome of World War II inspired many to pursue their own freedom. It was no accident that from 1951 to 1966, some three-quarters of African countries gained independence. Rwanda's quest began in the late 1950s; like many of the others, it was marked by bloodshed and turmoil.

Rwandans have had to live with the effects of war for many decades.

A Country Divided

Charles Rudahigwa Mutara III was the picture of a 20th century monarch. Standing six feet, eight inches (203 centimeters) tall, the Rwandan Mwami spoke fluent French and toured his country in a Lincoln convertible. Pleasing his Belgian colonial rulers, he not only converted to Catholicism, but also made it the national religion of Rwanda. Adored by both Tutsis and Hutus, in the 1950s it appeared he was helping to lead his country toward independence. But his sudden death at age forty-seven in late July of 1959 sparked the first of many violent conflicts.

By then, many Hutu were angry with the Tutsi. Tired of being given the worst jobs, enraged over high taxes, and most of all seeking a voice in the government, many Hutu pushed for independence even before Mutara III's death. When the late king's brother Kigeri V was crowned, the people were not supportive. By then, Belgium realized that if Rwanda became a true democracy—where everyone was allowed to vote—the Tutsi would be pushed from power. After all, they made up less than 10 percent of the population.

When the Hutu revolted against the Tutsi in November of 1959, they were assisted by the Belgian military. More than 150,000 Tutsis fled the country. In July of 1962, Ruanda-Urundi became two independent nations—Burundi and Rwanda.

Helicopters flew over villages, dropping leaflets explaining what independence would mean for the country. But instead of celebrating, many focused on revenge. "In Rwanda and Burundi the familiar African patterns can be plainly seen: migration followed by conquest, followed by... but here the sequence breaks down," write authors Marq de Villiers and Sheila Hirtle. "Here the migration and conquest was not followed by absorption at all, but by feudal rule, hatred, and genocide... More than anywhere else in Africa, the past poisons the present."[1]

The country's first elected president, Grégoire Kayibanda was the head of the Parmehutu (Party of the Hutu Emancipation Movement). Soon after he took power in 1962, strict quotas were introduced. Since Tutsis were 9 percent of the population, they could only take 9 percent of the government jobs. Schools could only be 9 percent Tutsi, and the rest of the students Hutu. Overnight, the school populations shifted. Over the next thirty years, violence continued and numerous Tutsi were killed both in Rwanda and Burundi.

In 1973, military commander Juvénal Habyarimana overthrew President Kayibanda. His rule marked a period of time during which Rwanda was essentially a dictatorship. Habyarimana expected to rule for life. Although there were elections, he was the only candidate to appear on voter ballots. Still, there were few riots or other uprisings during most of his time in office. Tensions between Hutus and Tutsis did increase, however.

A Tutsi-dominated group of Rwandan refugees called the Rwanda Patriotic Front (RPF) invaded the country from Uganda in 1990. For

FYI FACT:

Perhaps the most famous Rwandan in the world, thanks to his portrayal by the actor Don Cheadle in the film *Hotel Rwanda*, Paul Rusesabagina ran an elite hotel during the 1994 genocide. The son of a Hutu father and a Tutsi mother, for seventy-six days he protected over 1,200 people in his hotel. Although Hutus entered his hotel a number of times, he prevented them from harming anyone.

Juvénal Habyarimana

almost three years the country was engulfed in war. It was only a prelude.

On April 6, 1994, the plane carrying President Habyarimana and the president of Burundi was shot down. Almost immediately, the Rwandan military began killing those who had pushed for political change. Soon, numerous Hutus went after whatever Tutsis they could find, even as local radio stations encouraged them—proclaiming "the graves are not yet full."

Some of the Tutsi were killed by their neighbors, by people they knew. Many were murdered with machetes—very long knives—often by having their limbs cut off and being left to bleed to death. From the time of the plane crash until the RPF defeated the Rwandan army in mid-July, it is estimated that some 800,000 Tutsi were killed.

"Eight hundred thousand lives snuffed out in one hundred days," laments Rwandan Paul Rusesabagina. "That's eight thousand lives a

In 1994, Rwanda's Nyabarongo River served as a dumping ground for the bodies of many of the genocide victims.

United Nations peacekeeping vehicles headed for Rwanda in 1994.

day. More than five lives per minute. Every one of those lives was like a little world in itself. Some person who laughed and cried and ate and thought and felt and hurt just like any other person, just like you and me. A mother's child, every one irreplaceable."[2]

It was genocide—the mass murder of a group of people because of their race or ethnic background. There have been a number of genocides in the 20th century, but none killed so many people so quickly. In its aftermath, hundreds of thousands who had fled Rwanda remained in Zaire. The United States and numerous other countries provided aid to these refugees, while the United Nations peacekeeping forces remained in Rwanda until 1996.

Speaker of the Chamber of Parliament Rose Mukantabana is just one of many women in powerful government positions in Rwanda. In 2008, the country's parliament became the first in the world with a female majority.

Chapter 8

Modern Rwanda

Slowly, life in Rwanda improved. Over one million Rwandans returned to their country in 1996. The RPF-sponsored president, Paul Kagame, took office in 2000, and was officially elected in 2003. He was reelected in 2010 to serve another seven-year term. As head of state, the Rwandan president is commander of the armed forces and has a great deal of authority to administer policy. He can also declare war or a state of emergency.

In the 2000s, the Rwandan government replaced the country's flag, anthem, and constitution. The transitional constitution from 1994 was replaced following a national referendum in 2003.

Rwanda's Parliament operates much like the U.S. Congress. The lower chamber, The Chamber of Deputies, has eighty members while the upper chamber, the Senate, has twenty-six. The RPF is the dominant political party in Rwanda, although several other parties also hold seats in parliament.

In the new Rwanda, women are empowered to participate in the economy as well as the government. In 2008, the Parliament of Rwanda became the first in the world with a female majority. Laws have been revised, allowing women to inherit land, and offering them greater protection from domestic violence.

Some government programs instituted by the RPF have been very controversial. One program moved poor farmers from their land and into crowded villages. Forced to abandon their existing homes, many were not given new homes, and could only construct temporary

Many of those who survived Rwanda's genocide found themselves far from their homes, living in camps like this one.

shelters. The government's goal was to ensure access to police and security, which was more difficult to provide in rural areas. But many saw the new policies as a way for the RPF to gain more control over both the land and its people.

During the Kagame presidency, Rwanda has joined both the East African Community and the Commonwealth of Nations. These organizations consist of multiple countries working together to reach common goals such as world peace, improved healthcare, and free trade. Rwanda remains one of the most crowded countries in Africa and one of the poorest countries in the world. Still, tourism has greatly increased over the past decade.

For over twenty years, the United Nations has compiled a Human Development Index (HDI) which analyzes the health, education, and income of a country's people. Although Rwanda is ranked 166 out of

187 countries, its HDI has improved by over 30 percent in the past ten years.

Despite the country's successes, perhaps its biggest challenge is education. Although several small private universities have opened since the genocide, today very few Rwandans attend college. Indeed, in 2011, only 35 percent of high-school-aged children were enrolled in school.

Rwandan school children

In 2002, President Paul Kagame established traditional courts called *gacaca* ("on the grass") to try those suspected of involvement in the genocide. Some of the defendants approached the court in a non-traditional manner. Dressed in rose-colored prison uniforms, prior to the hearings many of them would dance and sing songs asking for forgiveness.

This is an improvement from 2001, however, when only 11 percent received any education past primary school.

During his time as president, Kagame has worked to bring together Tutsis, Hutus, and Twas. He has also brought about a number of reforms which have helped reduce poverty and have led to economic growth which is approaching 10 percent annually.

President Kagame

The National Liberation Day celebration at a Rwandan stadium

By 2001, over 100,000 were in prison for their role in the genocide. Only a small number of lawyers and judges were left in Rwanda after the genocide, so defendants waited years for trials. Many were eventually given sentences of jail time or public service.

Every year on April 7, known as Genocide Memorial Day, the country honors the dead in a ceremony commemorating the 1994 killings. On July 4, National Liberation Day honors the conclusion of the genocide with the RPF victory. On this occasion, people celebrate with parades, ceremonial drums, and dancers.

Peanut Nougat

Traditional meals in Rwanda use ingredients that are locally produced including bananas, sweet potatoes, corn, and goat. Like this sweet treat, most of them are fairly easy to produce.

Ingredients:
1   lb peanuts, shelled, and crushed or ground, if desired.
1½ c sugar
    Lemon juice, to taste

You will need:
A non-stick pan
A stove
A greased cookie sheet
A parent or adult's help

Directions:
1. Put the sugar in a non-stick pan and place on the stove's front burner. Begin to cook over medium heat. The sugar will melt and turn brown. Once it is a smooth syrup, remove the pan from the heat to avoid burning the nougat.
2. Slowly add the peanuts, stirring them in with a wooden spoon. When all of the peanuts have been added, squirt several drops of lemon juice over the mixture and continue to stir.
3. Now pour the contents of the pan onto the greased cookie sheet. Using the wooden spoon, pat down to about 1/4-inch thickness. Allow to cool—at least thirty minutes.
4. Cut or break into small squares and enjoy!

Traditional Sisal Basket

Today Hutu and Tutsi women have come together to weave baskets. These elaborate baskets are sold across the world. Although they can be bought in many major U.S. department stores, with a few simple items it is possible to make a similar basket using the techniques developed in Rwanda.

You will need:
Sisal rope (available at hardware stores)
Wood glue
A form in the shape and size you will
    make your basket
A binder clip
A paint brush
Oil-based paint
Scissors

Directions:

1. Start with a form to wrap the rope around—you can find foam in the shape of a basket at a craft store, or use a wire basket. The bottom of your form should be narrower than the top. Turn it upside down, placing the end of the rope in the center of the bottom of the basket. Use a binder clip or other type of clip to keep the rope in place.

2. Begin to wrap the rope in a circular pattern, until it is about 2 inches wide. Apply glue to the rope and allow to dry.

3. Once the glue is dry, continue to wrap the rope around the form, from the bottom to the top. At the upper-most point, apply more glue. Use scissors to cut the rope.

4. "Paint" glue along the rope over the entire basket, in the crevasses. Allow to set.

5. After the glue has dried, carefully remove the form you have used. Repeat the painting of the glue on the inside of the basket, and allow to dry.

6. Using paint, your basket can be decorated in a variety of patterns.

TIMELINE

B.C.E.

ca. 4,400,000 Hominids—the ancestors of human beings—live in parts of the Great Rift Valley stretching from the Afar Depression in the Northeast to the Omo Valley in the Southwest.

ca. 2,500,000 Stone tools are first used.

ca. 62,000 Bow and arrow first used by humans in modern-day South Africa.

**ca. 50,000-
20,000** Ancestors of the Twa live in the area around the rainforests of the Great Lakes Region, including Rwanda.

ca. 1000 Bantu farmers migrate across sub-Saharan Africa, including Rwanda.

C.E.

400s Hutu farmers arrive in Rwanda.

1300s The migration of Tutsis into Rwanda begins—they soon become the ruling power.

1600s Tutsi King Ruganzu Ndori subdues central Rwanda and establishes unified power.

1862 John Hanning Speke is the first European to encounter the Tutsis.

1885 The Berlin Conference divides Africa among the European nations; Rwanda becomes a part of German East Africa.

1894 German Count Gustav Adolf van Goetzen is the first European to explore what is now Rwanda.

1916 Belgians attack Rwanda from the Congo and oust the Germans.

1924 Rwanda becomes part of the Belgian-ruled protectorate Ruanda-Urundi under a League of Nations mandate.

1925 Albert National Park (now Virunga National Park and Volcanoes National Park), the first national park in Africa, is founded by the Belgian government in the Virunga Mountain Range to protect the mountain gorilla. Its boundary is expanded into Rwanda in 1929.

1933 The first identity cards for Tutsis and Hutus are issued by the Belgians.

1950 Polygamy is outlawed in Rwanda.

1959 Violence erupts following the death of Mwami Charles Rudahigwa Mutara III in July. In November, his successor Mwami Kigeri V flees the country along with over 150,000 Tutsis. George Schaller becomes the first scientist to study wild mountain gorillas in the Virunga Mountains.

1961 Rwanda becomes a republic, and The Party of the Hutu Emancipation Movement (Parmehutu) gains a majority of the seats in the National Assembly.

TIMELINE

1962 Ruanda-Urundi gains independence from Belgium, becoming the separate countries of Rwanda and Burundi. The Parmehutu leader, Grégoire Kayibanda, becomes the country's president.

1963 After Tutsis invade Rwanda from Burundi, Hutus respond by killing thousands of Tutsis.

1973 President Kayibanda is overthrown by General Juvénal Habyarimana.

1975 Rwanda becomes a single-party state with The National Revolutionary Movement for Development (MRND) as the sole party, and Habyarimana as its leader.

1978 Following an election where only the MRND is represented, President Habyarimana earns another five-year term.

1989 After the price of coffee declines, many in Rwanda face starvation. Although the International Monetary Fund agrees to help, the country must enact a number of reforms.

1990 Rwandan Tutsi refugees living in Uganda begin to attack Rwanda.

1991 Rwanda becomes a multiparty democracy.

1992 Park headquarters at Volcanoes National Park is attacked—the park is abandoned and tourist activities cease until 1999.

1994 After President Habyarimana's plane is shot down, Hutus begin attacking Tutsis. In just a few months, over 800,000 Tutsis are killed. The Tutsi refugee group Rwandan Patriotic Front (RPF) takes over leadership of Rwanda.

1996 Over one million refugees return to Rwanda.

1998 After Congolese President Kabila evicts Rwandan forces, Rwanda begins offering military support to groups trying to overthrow him.

2000 RPF member Paul Kagame is chosen as president by members of parliament.

2003 In the first election since the genocide, Kagame is elected president.

2004 The film *Hotel Rwanda* is released in the United States, detailing the true story of Rwandan hotel owner Paul Rusesabagina.

2008 Rwanda's Parliament becomes the first in the world with a female majority, including a female Speaker.

2010 Paul Kagame wins a second seven-year term as president.

2012 Rwandan gacaca courts are shut down after ten years of use.

Chapter 2. Native Animals
1. Kenneth LaPensee, "Reforestation." Ed. Brenda Wilmoth Lerner and K. Lee Lerner, *Environmental Science: In Context* (Detroit: Gale, 2009), p. 708.

Chapter 3. Beginnings
1. John Reader, *Africa* (Washington, D.C.: National Geographic Society, 2001), p. 29.
2. Ibid., p. 205.

Chapter 4. The People of Rwanda
1. John Reader, *Africa* (Washington, D.C.: National Geographic Society, 2001), pp. 96-98.

Chapter 5. Culture Beats
1. Gloria I. Anyango, *The New Times,* "Drumming the Sound of Success," September 28, 2009. http://www.newtimes.co.rw/news/index.php?a=20437&i=14032
2. Rosamond Halsey Carr and Ann Howard Halsey, *Land of a Thousand Hills: My Life in Rwanda* (New York: Viking, 1999), p. 78.

Chapter 6. Arrival of the Colonials
1. John Hanning Speke, *Journal of the Discovery of the Source of the Nile* (London: Everyman Edition, 1969), p. 202.
2. John Reader, *Africa: A Biography of the Continent* (New York: A.A. Knopf, 1998), p. 531.

Chapter 7. A Country Divided
1. Marq de Villiers and Sheila Hirtle, *Into Africa* (Toronto, Ontario: Key Porter Books, 1997), p. 358.
2. Paul Rusesabagina and Tom Zoellner, *An Ordinary Man: An Autobiography* (New York: Viking, 2006), p. xi.

Abacus Uganda Safaris: "Rwanda Safari Parks." http://www.ugandansafari.com/
  rwanda-safari-parks

Anyango, Gloria I. "Drumming the Sound of Success," *The New Times,* September
  28, 2009. http://www.newtimes.co.rw/news/index.php?a=20437&i=14032

BBC News Africa. *Rwanda Profile:* "A Chronology of Key Events." http://news.
  bbc.co.uk/2/hi/africa/1070329.stm

Carr, Rosamond Halsey, and Ann Howard Halsey. *Land of a Thousand Hills: My
  Life in Rwanda.* New York: Viking, 1999.

De la Bédoyère, Camilla, and Dian Fossey. *No One Loved Gorillas More: Dian
  Fossey, Letters From the Mist.* Washington, D.C.: National Geographic, 2005.

De Villiers, Marq, and Sheila Hirtle. *Into Africa: A Journey Through the Ancient
  Empires.* Toronto, Ontario: Key Porter Books, 1997.

Hayes, Harold. *The Dark Romance of Dian Fossey.* New York: Simon and Schuster,
  1990.

LaPensee, Kenneth. "Reforestation." Brenda Wilmoth Lerner and K. Lee Lerner,
  Eds. *Environmental Science: In Context.* Vol. 2. Detroit: Gale, 2009.

Lynn, Stephanie. *Under the Table and Dreaming:* "Make Your Own Natural Fiber
  Sisal Rope Basket," February 10, 2011. http://www.bystephanielynn.
  com/2011/02/make-your-own-natural-fiber-sisal-rope.html

McCrummen, Stephanie. "Women Run the Show In a Recovering Rwanda." *The
  Washington Post,* October 27, 2008. http://www.washingtonpost.com/wp-dyn/
  content/article/2008/10/26/AR2008102602197_2.html?sid=ST2008051504314

Naipaul, V. S. *The Masque of Africa: Glimpses of African Belief.* New York: Alfred A.
  Knopf, 2010.

PBS Frontline: "Rwanda: A Historical Chronology." http://www.pbs.org/wgbh/
  pages/frontline/shows/rwanda/etc/cron.html

Reader, John. *Africa: A Biography of the Continent.* New York: A.A. Knopf, 1998.

Reader, John. *Africa.* Washington, D.C.: National Geographic Society, 2001.

Rusesabagina, Paul, and Tom Zoellner. *An Ordinary Man: An Autobiography.* New
  York: Viking, 2006.

"Rwanda—Inyange—Traditional Drummers," YouTube video. Uploaded by
  idamawat on December 3, 2008. http://www.youtube.com/
  watch?v=m2JnkzY1eLY

"Rwandan Dance and Drums." YouTube video. Uploaded by Sean Obedih on
  May 14, 2007. http://www.youtube.com/watch?v=coLwczB5L3U

The Official Website of Rwanda Tourism: "Welcome to Rwanda." http://www.
  rwandatourism.com

Thurow, Roger, and Scott Kilman. *Enough: Why the World's Poorest Starve in an Age
  of Plenty.* New York: PublicAffairs, 2009.

UNESCO World Heritage Centre: "Virunga National Park." http://whc.unesco.
  org/en/list/63

United Nations International Human Development Indicators: "Rwanda Country
  Profile." http://hdrstats.undp.org/en/countries/profiles/RWA.html

Visonà, Monica Blackmun. *A History of Art in Africa.* New York: Harry N.
  Abrams, 2001.

Weavings from Rwanda: "Women Work to Weave a Lasting Peace." http://www.
  oneworldprojects.com/products/rwandan_weaving.shtml

Weber, Bill, and Amy Vedder. *In the Kingdom of Gorillas: Fragile Species in a
  Dangerous Land.* New York: Simon & Schuster, 2001.

FURTHER READING AND GLOSSARY

Books

Matthews, Tom. *Light Shining Through the Mist: A Photobiography of Dian Fossey.* Washington D.C.: National Geographic Society, 1998.

Streissguth, Thomas. *Rwanda in Pictures.* Minneapolis: Lerner, 2008.

Turner, Pamela S. *Gorilla Doctors: Saving Endangered Great Apes.* Boston: Houghton Mifflin Co., 2005.

Twagilimana, Aimable. *Hutu and Tutsi.* New York: Rosen, 1997.

On the Internet

African Wildlife Foundation: "Golden Monkeys"
   http://www.awf.org/content/solution/detail/3509

African Wildlife Foundation: "Mountain Gorilla"
   http://www.awf.org/content/wildlife/detail/mountaingorilla

Archaeologyinfo.com: "Homo sapiens"
   http://archaeologyinfo.com/homo-sapiens/

BBC: Wildlife, "Eastern Gorilla"
   http://www.bbc.co.uk/nature/life/Eastern_Gorilla

Institute of National Museums of Rwanda
   http://www.museum.gov.rw/

National Geographic: "Mountain Gorilla"
   http://animals.nationalgeographic.com/animals/mammals/mountain-gorilla/

Rwanda Development Board: *Kwita Izina* (Gorilla Naming Ceremony)
   http://www.rdb.rw/kwitizina/

"Silverback Mountain Gorilla Charging in Rwanda," YouTube video.
   http://www.youtube.com/watch?v=pPT4wybjHH0

GLOSSARY

anthropologist (an-thra-POL-uh-jist): A scientist who studies human beings and their ancestors.

arid (AIR-id): Very dry and not having enough rainfall for farming.

fossil (FAHS-ull): The remains of a living creature preserved in the earth's crust.

paleontologist (pay-lee-ahn-TOL-uh-jist): A scientist who studies ancient life using fossils.

republic (ree-PUB-lik): Government whose chief of state is not a monarch; the greatest power rests with citizens who vote for their representatives.

savanna (suh-VAN-ah): Grasslands with few trees.

vegetarian (vej-ah-TAIR-ee-uhn): Person or animal who does not eat meat.

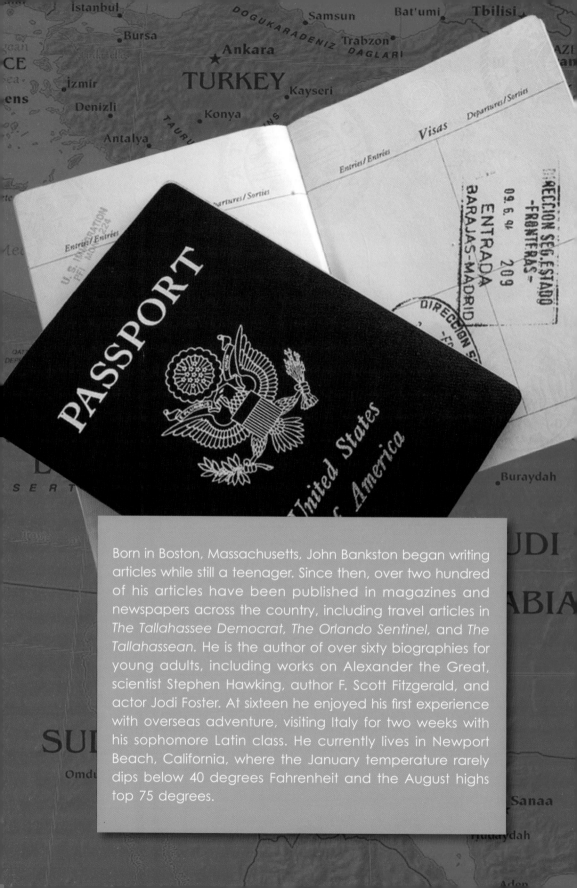

Born in Boston, Massachusetts, John Bankston began writing articles while still a teenager. Since then, over two hundred of his articles have been published in magazines and newspapers across the country, including travel articles in *The Tallahassee Democrat, The Orlando Sentinel,* and *The Tallahassean.* He is the author of over sixty biographies for young adults, including works on Alexander the Great, scientist Stephen Hawking, author F. Scott Fitzgerald, and actor Jodi Foster. At sixteen he enjoyed his first experience with overseas adventure, visiting Italy for two weeks with his sophomore Latin class. He currently lives in Newport Beach, California, where the January temperature rarely dips below 40 degrees Fahrenheit and the August highs top 75 degrees.